D0330887

Acres of Diamonds

Acres of Diamonds

Russell Conwell's Inspiring

Classic About Opportunity

Edited for Contemporary Readers

By William R. Webb

With Drawings by Betty Fraser

Hallmark Editions

Copyright © 1968 by Hallmark Cards Inc.,
Kansas City, Missouri. All Rights Reserved.
Printed in the United States of America.
Library of Congress Catalog Card Number: 68-19596.

THE DRAMATIC ORIGINS
OF » ACRES OF DIAMONDS «

Few essays have attracted as much attention or inspired as much enduring interest as *Acres of Diamonds*. Its author, Russell H. Conwell, delivered it as a public lecture more than 6,000 times from 1877 until his death in 1925. In book form it has been a popular American classic since it first saw print. Conwell himself earned several million dollars from it. True to its message, he gave away every penny to help thousands of young people receive college educations.

Acres of Diamonds is a remarkable essay. It offers every reader a practical formula for wealth and happiness. It argues fervently that riches and success are respectable and admirable pursuits—pursuits sanctioned by Christianity as well as by their immense power for good. It proves its point with fascinating true stories of spiritual and financial success—and failure. Its principles are profoundly American, starting with that most American principle of all, "Every man can be more than he is."

Russell Conwell exemplified the principles he proclaimed. During his long life he was, variously, a soldier, school teacher, newspaper correspondent, lawyer, lecturer, Baptist minister, and the founder of Temple University in Philadelphia, Pennsylvania.

Born in 1843 in the Eastern Berkshire mountains of Massachusetts, Conwell grew up among hardy New Englanders who wrested a living from the rocky land. His father's fanatic religious attitudes affected the young man negatively.

"I was filled with awe, dread, and fear," he said later of his feelings toward his father, "until I decided to fight with all my power. . . . I became an atheist, or at least I thought I was one."

He did not long remain so. He was transformed by a harrowing war experience.

In the fall of 1862, young Conwell organized and was elected captain of a Massachusetts militia company that would see battle in the American Civil War. Apparently his personality was already magnetic, because not long after the militia's organization, members of his company presented him with an ornate sword. The sword bore a Latin inscription on the blade: "True friendship is eternal."

The company went to war. An eager youth named John Ring signed on as Conwell's aide. Ring soon idolized Conwell even though Conwell refused to allow the boy to read the Bible. He was appointed keeper of the sword, which was too decorative to be worn in battle. Ring kept it polished and hanging on his captain's tent pole.

One morning near New Bern, North Carolina, Confederate forces swept through Conwell's camp. He and his company were driven into retreat across the Neuse River where a rear guard of Union soldiers hastily set fire to the long covered bridge behind them.

Unknown to his captain, John Ring had returned to the tent to save the prized sword. When he ran back to the bridge, he found the structure blazing from end to end. Still he started across.

Gunfire ceased from both sides as the young soldier struggled across the burning timbers. A Confederate officer called to Ring to jump into the water below. Ring didn't hear, or didn't heed. Smoke enveloped the bridge's covered section. He vanished into it.

Northerner and Southerner waited for tense minutes in silence, their guns stilled. Then a shout went up as Ring crawled from the Union end of the bridge, his clothes blazing. He tried to stand but staggered and fell into the shallow water at the edge of the river—still clutching the sword.

John Ring died soon afterward in a Union hospital. His sacrifice made such an impression on Russell Conwell that he vowed he would devote the rest of his life to the service of his fellowmen. He always kept the sword hanging above his bed. As Dr. Conwell explained, "This is to remind me each morning when I rise that I must live two lives that day—my own and that of Johnny Ring."

The inspiration for *Acres of Diamonds* dates to a trip young Conwell took as a foreign correspondent for the New York *Tribune* and the Boston *Traveler*. A Turkish guide on the Tigris River told him the story of Ali Hafed, a Persian farmer who died a pauper because he wasted his life searching for wealth. Not long after the man's death, diamonds were discovered on his own land. For most of the tourists, the story was only another legend. But to Russell Conwell, it meant, "Your diamonds are not in far-distant mountains or in yonder seas; they are in your own backyard, if you but dig for them." So Russell Conwell returned to America, eventually became an ordained minister, and began the work which led to the founding of Temple University.

He first delivered *Acres of Diamonds* as an address at a reunion of his regiment a decade after the Civil War. It would be a constant companion for all his remaining years, years when he found deep religious belief and a profound dedication to education. Crowds flocked to hear the distinguished veteran, minister, and educator wherever he went. He turned their gifts to great charitable advantage, following his own principle that "money is power, and you should be reasonably ambitious to have it." Because, he continues, "*you can do more good with it* than you could without it."

But money is not really Russell Conwell's central subject in *Acres of Diamonds*. The real message of the essay, dramatized time and again with true stories, is that opportunity abounds in every backyard, in every city, on every farm, if only you study that opportunity and create it yourself. Acquiring wealth can be the result of one kind of opportunity; helping others, of another. Russell Conwell, converted by the dedication of a young soldier, did both. In *Acres of Diamonds* he shares his most inspiring secrets.

ACRES OF DIAMONDS

While traveling down the Tigris and Euphrates rivers many years ago, I found myself in the company of an old Arab guide we had hired at Bagdad. He was unusually talkative and seemed to think it was not only his duty to guide us, and do what he was paid for doing, but also to entertain us with stories.

The old guide, who was leading my camel along the river bank toward Nineveh, told me story after story until I grew weary and ceased to listen. I remember that he took off his Turkish cap and swung it in a circle to get my attention. I could see it through the corner of my eye, but I had decided not to look at him for fear he would begin again. I finally did look, nevertheless, and as soon as I did he went right into another story.

He said, "I will tell you a story now which I reserve for my particular friends." When he emphasized the words "particular friends," I listened, and I have always been glad I did.

The old guide told me that there once lived not far from the River Indus an ancient Persian by the name of Ali Hafed. He said that Ali Hafed owned a very large farm, that he had orchards, grain fields, and gardens, and that he had money. He was a wealthy and contented man. He was contented because he was wealthy, and wealthy because he was contented.

One day an ancient Buddhist priest, one of the wise men of the East, visited that old Persian farmer. He sat down by the fire and told the old farmer how this world of ours was made. He said that it was once a bank of fog, and that the Almighty thrust His finger into the fog, and began slowly to move His finger around, increasing the speed until at last He whirled the bank of fog into a solid ball of fire. Then it went rolling through the universe, burning its way through other banks of fog, and condensed the moisture without, until it fell in floods of rain upon its hot surface, and cooled the outward crust. Then the internal fires burst outward through the crust throwing up the mountains and hills, the valleys, the plains and prairies of this wonderful world of ours. As this internal molten mass came bursting out, that part which cooled quickly became granite; less quickly copper, less quickly silver, less quickly gold, and, after gold, diamonds were made.

The Creation of Diamonds
The old priest said, "A diamond is a congealed drop of sunlight." The old priest told Ali Hafed that if he

had a diamond the size of his thumb he could purchase the county, and if he had a mine of diamonds he could place his children upon thrones through the influence of his great wealth.

Ali Hafed heard all about diamonds, how much they were worth, and went to bed that night a poor man. He had not lost anything, but he was poor because he was discontented, and discontented because he feared he was poor. He said, "I want a mine of diamonds," and he lay awake all night.

Early in the morning he sought out the priest. Ali Hafed said to him:

"Will you tell me where I can find diamonds?"

"Diamonds! What do you want with diamonds?" asked the priest. "Why, I wish to be immensely rich." said Ali Hafed.

"Well,then, go along and find them. That is all you have to do; go and find them, and then you have them."

"But I don't know where to go," Ali Hafed replied.

"Well, if you will find a river that runs through white sands, between high mountains, in those white sands you will always find diamonds."

"I don't believe there is any such river."

"Oh yes, there are plenty of them. All you have to do is to go and find them, and then you have them."

"I will go," said Ali Hafed.

11

To The Mountains of the Moon

So he sold his farm, collected his money, left his family in charge of a neighbor, and went in search of diamonds. He began his search, very properly to my mind, at the Mountains of the Moon in Kenya. Afterward he went to Palestine, then wandered on into Europe, and at last when his money was all spent and he was wretched and in rags, he stood upon the shore at Barcelona, Spain, when a great tidal wave came rolling in between the pillars of Hercules. The poor, afflicted, suffering, dying man could not resist the awful temptation to cast himself into that incoming tide, and he sank beneath its foaming crest, never to rise in this life again.

When that old guide had finished this part of his story, he stopped the camel I was riding and went back to fix some baggage that was coming off another camel. I remember saying to myself, "Why did he reserve that story for his 'particular friends'?" There seemed to be no beginning, no middle, and end, nothing to it. That was the first story I had heard in my life in which the hero was killed in the first chapter.

Black Eye of Light

When the guide came back and took up the halter of my camel, he went right into the second chapter of the story, just as though there had been no break.

The man who purchased Ali Hafed's farm led his camel into the garden to drink one day, and as the animal put its nose into the shallow water of the garden brook, Ali Hafed's successor noticed a curious flash of light from the white sands of the stream. He pulled out a black stone which had an eye of light reflecting all the hues of the rainbow. He took the stone into the house and put it on the mantel which covers the central fires, and forgot about it.

A few days later the old Buddhist priest came to visit Ali Hafed's successor, and the moment he opened that drawing-room door he saw a flash of light on the mantel, and he rushed up to it, and shouted: "Here is a diamond! Has Ali Hafed returned?"

"Oh no, Ali Hafed has not returned, and that is not a diamond. That is nothing but a stone we found out in our garden," said Ali Hafed's successor.

"But," said the priest, "I tell you I know a diamond when I see it. I know positively that is a diamond."

Then together they rushed out into that old garden and stirred up the white sands with their fingers, and there came up other more beautiful and valuable gems than the first.

"Thus," said the guide to me, "was discovered the diamond mine of Golconda, the most magnificent diamond mine in all the history of mankind, excell-

ing the Kimberly itself. The Kohinoor of the crown jewels of England, once the largest on earth, the great blue Hope diamond, and the famous Regent diamond came from that mine."

When the old Arab guide had finished the second chapter of his story, he took off his Turkish cap and swung it around in the air again to attract my attention before telling the moral. Arab guides have morals to their stories. As he swung his hat, he said to me, "Had Ali Hafed remained at home and dug in his own cellar, or underneath his own wheat field, or in his own garden, he would have had 'acres of diamonds.' For every acre of that old farm, yes, every shovelful, afterward revealed gems which since have decorated the crowns of monarchs."

When he had added the moral to his story I saw why he reserved it for his "particular friends." But I did not tell him I could see it. It was that old Arab's way of saying indirectly what he did not dare say directly, that "in his opinion there was a certain young man then traveling down the Tigris River that might better be at home in America." I did not tell him I could see that, but I told him his story reminded me of one.

A Passion for Gold

I told him of a man in California in 1847, who owned a ranch. He heard they had discovered gold in

Southern California, and so with a passion for gold he sold his ranch to Colonel Sutter, and away he went, never to come back. Colonel Sutter put a mill upon a stream that ran through that ranch, and one day his little girl brought some wet sand from the raceway into their home and sifted it through her fingers before the fire. In that falling sand a visitor saw the first shining scales of real gold discovered in California.

The man who had owned that ranch wanted gold, and he could have had it for the taking. Indeed, thirty-eight million dollars worth has been taken out of a very few acres since then. Some time ago I was in the city that stands on that farm, and was told a one-third owner had been getting one hundred and twenty dollars in gold from that land every fifteen minutes, night and day.

But what makes a better illustration than that occurred in Pennsylvania. There was a man living in Pennsylvania who owned a farm, and he sold it. But before he sold it he decided he would collect coal oil for his cousin, who was in the business in Canada. So this Pennsylvania farmer wrote to his cousin asking for employment.

You see, friends, this farmer was not altogether a foolish man. No, he was not. He did not leave his farm until he had something else to do.

When he wrote to his cousin for employment, his

cousin replied, "I cannot hire you because you know nothing about the oil business."

Well, then the farmer said, "I will learn," and with commendable zeal he studied the whole subject. He began back at the second day of God's creation when the world was covered thick and deep with that rich vegetation which since has turned into beds of coal. He studied the subject until he found that the drainings of those rich beds of coal furnished the coal oil that was worth pumping, and then he found how it came up with living springs. He studied until he knew what it looked like, smelled like, tasted like, and how to refine it. Then he said in a letter to his cousin, "I understand the oil business." His cousin answered, "All right, come on."

So he sold his farm, according to the county record, for $833. He was scarcely gone before the man who purchased the place went out to water his cattle. He found the previous owner had put a plank in the brook back of the barn. The plank was set in the water so it would throw a dreadful-looking scum onto the bank. With the plank there, cattle could drink below. Thus the man who had gone to Canada had been damming a flood of coal oil which state geologists in Pennsylvania later declared was worth a billion dollars.

The man who owned that territory on which the city of Titusville now stands, and those Pleasantville valleys, had studied the subject from the second day of God's creation clear down to the present time. He studied it until he knew all about it, and yet he is said to have sold the whole of it for $833, and "no sense."

But I need another illustration. I found it in Massachusetts, and I am sorry I did because that is the state I came from. This young man in Massachusetts furnishes just another phase of my thought. He went to Yale College and studied mines and mining, and became such an adept as a mining engineer that he was employed by the authorities of the university to train students who were behind their classes. During his senior year he earned $15 a week for doing that work. When he graduated they raised his pay from $15 to $45 a week and offered him a professorship, and as soon as they did he went right home to his mother. *If they had raised that boy's pay from $15 to $15.60 he would have stayed and been proud of the place, but when they put it up to $45 at one leap, he said, "Mother, I won't work for $45 a week. The idea of a man with a brain like mine working for $45 a week! Let's go out in California and stake out gold mines and silver mines, and be immensely rich."*

Said his mother, "Now, Charlie, it is just as well to be happy as it is to be rich."

"Yes," said Charlie, "but it is just as well to be rich and happy, too." And they were both right about it.

As he was an only son and she a widow, of course he had his way. They always do.

They sold out in Massachusetts, and instead of going to California they went to Wisconsin, where he went into the employ of the Superior Copper Mining Company at $15 a week again, but with the proviso in his contract that he should have an interest in any mines he should discover for the company. I don't believe he ever discovered a mine.

But I do know the other end of the line. He had scarcely gotten out of the old homestead before the succeeding owner went out to dig potatoes. The potatoes were already growing in the ground when he bought the farm, and as the old farmer was bringing in a basket of potatoes it hugged very tight between the ends of the stone fence. You know in Massachusetts our farms are nearly all stone wall. There you are obliged to be very economical of front gateways in order to have some place to put the stone. When this basket hugged so tight he set it down on the ground, and then dragged on one side, and pulled on the other side, and as he was dragging that basket through this farmer noticed in the upper and outer corner of the stone wall, right next to the gate, a block of native silver eight inches square. That professor of mines, mining, and mineralogy, who knew so much about the subject that he would not work for $45 a week, when he sold that homestead in Massachusetts sat right on that silver to make the bargain. He was born on that homestead, was brought up there, and had gone back and forth rubbing the stone with his sleeve until it reflected his countenance, and seemed to say, "Here is a hundred thousand dollars right down here just for the taking." But he would not take it. It was in a home in Newburyport, Massachusetts, and there was no silver there, all away off—well, I don't know where, and he did not, but somewhere else, and he was a professor of mineralogy.

My friends, that mistake is very universally made. Why should we even smile at him? I often wonder

what has become of him. I do not know at all, but I will tell you what I "guess" as a Yankee. I guess that he sits out there by his fireside tonight with his friends gathered around him, and he is saying to them something like this: "Do you know that man Jones who lives in Philadelphia?" "Yes, I have heard of him, too."

Then he begins to laugh, and shakes his sides, and says to his friends, "Well, they have done just the same thing I did, precisely"—and that spoils the whole joke, for you and I have done the same thing he did, and while we laugh at him he has a better right to sit out there and laugh at us. I know I have made the same mistakes, but, of course, that does not make any difference, because we don't expect the same man to preach and practice, too.

I was greatly interested in an account in the newspaper of a young man who found a diamond in North Carolina. It was one of the purest diamonds that has ever been discovered, and it has several predecessors near the same locality. I went to a distinguished professor in mineralogy and asked him where he thought those diamonds came from. The professor secured the map of the geologic formations of our continent, and traced it. He said it went either through the underlying carboniferous strata adapted for such production, westward through Ohio and the Mississippi, or in more probability came eastward through Virginia and up the shore of the Atlantic Ocean. It is a fact that the diamonds were there, for they have been discovered and sold; and that they were carried down there during the drift period, from some northern locality. Now who can say but some person going down with his drill in his home town will find some trace of a diamond mine yet down there? Oh, friends! you cannot say that you are not over one of the greatest diamond mines in the world, for such a diamond as that only comes from the most profitable mines that are found on earth.

Wealth Where You Live

My friends, these stories are universal. So I say to you that you have "acres of diamonds" right where you now live.

As I go out lecturing and look around the audiences, I see again and again what, through the long years of my life, I have continually seen—men who are making precisely the same mistake. I often wish that the lecture halls were filled every night with high school scholars and grammar school scholars, so that I could have them to talk to. I would prefer such an audience because they are most susceptible, as they have not grown up into their prejudices as adults have, they have not gotten into any custom that they cannot break, they have not met with any failures as adults have. I believe my point is one which the young especially should take to heart. I could perhaps do the young more good than I can do grown-up people. Yet I try to do the best with the material I have, young or old. All of us can profit from a new way of thinking about things.

"Oh," but you will say, "you cannot know much about our city if you think there are any 'acres of diamonds' here."

Now then, I say again that the opportunity to get rich, to attain unto great wealth, is here now, within the reach of almost every man and woman who hears me speak tonight, and I mean just what I say. I am not here to recite something to you. I am here to tell you what in God's sight I believe to be the truth, and if the years of life have been of any value to me in the attainment of common sense, I know I am right; that the men and women here have within their reach "acres of diamonds," opportunities to get largely wealthy. There never was a place on earth more adapted than this city today, and never in the history of the world did a poor man without capital have such an opportunity to get rich quickly and honestly as he has now. I say it is the truth, and I want you to accept it as such; for if you think I have come to simply recite something, then I would better not be here. I have no time to waste in any such talk, but to say the things that I believe, and unless some of you get richer for what I am saying my time is wasted.

I say that you ought to get rich, and it is your duty to get rich.

Many of my brethren say to me, "Do you, a Christian minister, spend your time going up and down the country advising young people to get rich, to get money?"

"Yes, of course I do."

They say, "Isn't that awful! Why don't you preach the gospel instead of preaching about man making money?"

"Because to make money honestly is to preach the gospel." That is the reason. The men who get rich may be the most honest men you find in the community.

"Oh," a young man says, "but I have been told that if a person has money he is dishonest and contemptible."

My friend, that is the reason why you have none, because you have that idea. The foundation of your faith is altogether false. Let me say here clearly, and say it briefly: Ninety-eight out of one hundred of the rich men of America are honest. That is why they are rich. That is why they are trusted with money. That is why they carry on great enterprises and find people to work with them. It is because they are honest men.

Another young man says, "I hear some men get millions of dollars dishonestly."

Yes, of course you do, and so do I. But they are so rare that the newspapers talk about them all the time, until you get the idea that all rich men got rich dishonestly.

Money Is Power

Take me out into the suburbs. Introduce me to the people who own their homes, those beautiful homes with gardens and flowers, those magnificent homes so lovely in their art, and I will introduce you to the very best people in character as well as in enterprise in our city, and you know I will. A man is not really a true man until he owns his own home, and they that own their homes are made more honorable and honest and pure, and true and economical and careful, by owning the home.

For a man to have money, even in large sums, is not an inconsistent thing. We preach against covetousness so extremely that Christians get the idea that when we stand in the pulpit we believe it is wicked for any man to have money—until the collection-basket comes around.

Money is power, and you should be reasonably ambitious to have it. You should because you can do more good with it than you could without it. Money prints your Bible, money builds your churches, money sends your missionaries, and money pays your preachers, and you would not have many of them, either, if you did not pay them.

I say, then, you should have money. If you can honestly attain riches, it is your Christian and godly duty to do so. It is a mistake of these pious people to think you must be poor in order to be pious.

A gentleman says, "Don't you think there are things in this world that are better than money?"

Of course I do, but I am talking about money now. Oh yes, I know that there are things in this world that are higher and sweeter and purer than money. Love is the grandest thing on God's earth, but fortunate the lover who has plenty of money. Money is power, money is force, money will do good as well as harm. In the hands of good men and women it could accomplish, and it has accomplished, good.

Misplaced Piety

Yet the age is prejudiced against advising a man to attain wealth. The prejudice is so universal and the years are far enough back, I think, for me to mention that years ago at Temple University there was a young man in our theological school who thought he was the only pious student in the department.

He came into my office one evening and sat down by my desk, and said to me, "Mr. President, I think it is my duty, Sir, to come in and talk to you."

"What has happened?" I asked.

He said, "I heard you say that you thought it was an honorable ambition for a young man to desire wealth, and that you thought it made him temperate, made him anxious to have a good name, and made him industrious. You spoke about man's ambition to have money helping to make him a good man. Sir, I have come to tell you the Holy Bible says that money is the root of all evil.' "

I said I had never seen it in the Bible, and told him to go out into the chapel and get the Bible, and show me the place. So out he went for the Bible, and soon he stalked into my office with the Bible open.

"Now please read the passage," I said, " and give it the emphasis it deserves."

He read, " 'The *love of* money is the root of all evil.' "

Suddenly he understood as one does when he quotes that old Book right. "The love of money is the root of all evil." He who tries to attain it too quickly, or dishonestly, will fall into many snares, no doubt about that.

The love of money. What is that? It is making an idol of money, and idolatry pure and simple everywhere is condemned by the Holy Scriptures and by man's common sense. The man who worships the dollar instead of thinking of the purposes for which it ought to be used, the man who idolizes money, the miser who hoards his money in the cellar, or hides it in his stocking, or refuses to invest it where it will do the world good, the man who hugs the dollar until the eagle squeals has in him the root of all evil.

A Measure of Man's Worth

I think now I will answer the question nearly all of you are asking: "Is there opportunity today for anyone to get rich?" Well, now, how simple a thing it is to see that there is, and the instant you see it is, it is yours.

An old gentleman says, "Mr. Conwell, the time has gone by when you can make anything in this city."

"No, I don't think it has."

"Yes, it has; I have tried it."

"What business are you in?"

"I kept a store here for twenty years, and never made over a thousand dollars in the whole twenty years."

"Well, then, you can measure the good you have been to this city by what this city has paid you. That's because a man can judge very well what he is worth by what he receives. If you have not made over a thousand dollars in twenty years, it would have been better if they had kicked you out of the city nineteen years and nine months ago. A man has no right to keep a store twenty years and not make at least five hundred thousand dollars, even though it be a corner grocery."

You say, "You can't even make five thousand dollars in a store now."

Oh, my friends, if you will look only four blocks

around you, and find out what the people want and what you can supply, and figure up the profits you would make, you would very soon see it. There is wealth right within the sound of your voice.

Someone says, "You don't know anything about business. A preacher never knows a thing about business."

An Expert By Experience

Well, then, I will have to prove that I am an expert. I don't like to do this, but I have to do it because my testimony will not be valid if I am not an expert. My father kept a country store, and if there is any place under the stars where a man gets all sorts of experience in every kind of mercantile transaction, it is in the country store. I am not proud of my experience, but sometimes when my father was away he would leave me in charge of the store, though fortunately for him it was not very often.

A man would come in the store, and say to me, "Do you keep jackknives?"

"No, we don't keep jackknives," and I went off whistling a tune. What did I care about that man, anyhow?

Then another would come in and say, "Do you keep jackknives?"

"No, we don't keep jackknives." Then I went away and whistled another tune.

Then a third man came in the same door and said, "Do you keep jackknives?"

"No. Why is everyone around here asking for jackknives? Do you suppose we are keeping this store to supply the whole neighborhood with jack-knives?"

Do you carry on your store like that? The difficulty was I had not then learned that the foundation of godliness and the foundation of success in business are both the same.

The man who says, "I cannot carry my religion into business," advertises himself either as being an imbecile, on the road to bankruptcy, or a thief, one of the three. He will fail within a few years. He certainly will if he doesn't carry his religion into business.

If I had been running my father's store on a Christian plan, godly plan, I would have had a jackknife for the third man when he called for it. Then I would have actually done him a kindness, and I would have received a reward myself, which it would have been my duty to take.

There are some over-pious Christians who think if you take any profit on anything that you are an unrighteous man. On the contrary, it would be criminal to sell goods for less than they cost. You have no right to do that. You cannot trust a man with your money who cannot take care of his own.

You cannot trust a man in your family who is not true to his own wife. You cannot trust a man in the world who does not begin with his own heart, his own character, and his own life.

The Law and the Profit

It would have been my duty to have furnished a jackknife to the third man, or the second, and to have sold it to him and actually profited myself. I have no more right to sell goods without making a profit than I have to overcharge him dishonestly beyond that they are worth. But I should so sell that the person to whom I sell shall make as much as I.

To live and let live is the principle of the gospel, and the principle of everyday common sense. Oh, young man, hear me; live as you go along. Do not wait until you have reached my years before you begin to enjoy anything of this life. If I had the millions back, or fifty cents of it, which I have tried to earn in these years, it would not do me anything like the good that it does me now in speaking here. Oh, yes, I am paid over and over a hundredfold for dividing as I have tried to do in some measure as I went along through the years. I ought not speak that way, it sounds egotistic, but I am old enough now to be excused for that. I should have helped my fellow men, which I have tried to do, and everyone should try to do, and get the happiness of it.

The man who goes home with the sense that he has stolen a dollar, that he has robbed a man of what was his honest due, is not going home to sweet rest. He arises tired in the morning, and goes with an unclean conscience to his work. He is not a successful man at all, although he may have laid up millions. But the man who has gone through life dividing always with his fellowmen, making and demanding his own rights and his own profits, and giving to every other man his rights and profits, lives every day, and not only that, he is on the road to great wealth. The history of thousands of millionaires shows this to be the case.

The man who said he could not make anything in a store has been running his store on the wrong principle. Suppose I go into his store tomorrow morning and ask, "Do you know neighbor A, who lives one block away, at house No. 1240?"

"Oh yes, I have met him," he may reply. "He deals here at the corner store."

"Where did he come from?"

"I don't know."

"How many does he have in his family?"

"I don't know."

"What ticket does he vote?"

"I don't know."

"What church does he go to?"

"I don't know, and don't care. "

'If You Had Cared. . . .'

If you had a store would you answer me like that? If so, then you are conducting your business just as I carried on my father's business in Worthington, Massachusetts. You don't know where your neighbor came from, and you don't care. If you had cared you would be a rich man now. If you had cared enough about him to take an interest in his affairs, to find out what he needed, you would have been rich. But you go through the world saying, "No opportunity to get rich," and there is the fault right at your own door.

But another young man says, "I cannot go into the mercantile business."

"Why can't you go into the mercantile business?"

"Because I haven't any capital."

"Young man, do you think you are going to get rich on capital?"

"Certainly."

The Burden of Capital

Well, I say, "Certainly not." The moment a young man or woman gets more money than he or she can handle through practical experience, that moment he or she is cursed. It is no help to a young man or woman to inherit money. It is no help to your children to leave them money, but if you leave them education, if you leave them Christian and noble character, if you leave them a wide circle of friends, if you leave them an honorable name, it is far better than money.

Young man, if you have inherited money, don't regard it as a help. It will curse you through your years, and deprive you of the best things of human life. There is no class of people to be pitied so much as the inexperienced sons and daughters of the rich of our generation. I pity the rich man's son. He can never know the best things in life.

One of the best things in our life is when a young man has earned his own living, and when he becomes engaged to some lovely young woman, and makes up his mind to have a home of his own. Then with that same love comes also that divine inspiration toward better things, and he begins to save his money. He begins to leave off his bad habits and put money in the bank. When he has a few hundred dollars he goes out in the suburbs to look for a home. He goes to the savings bank, perhaps, for half of the value, and then goes for his wife, and when he takes his bride over the threshold of that door for the first time he says in words of eloquence my voice can never touch: "I have earned this home myself. It is all mine, and I divide with thee." That is the grandest moment a human heart may ever know.

Statistics show that not one rich man's son out of seventeen ever dies rich. I pity the rich man's sons unless they have the good sense of Cornelius Vanderbilt's son, which sometimes happens.

He went to his father and said, "Did you earn all your money?"

"I did, my son. I began by working on a ferryboat for twenty-five cents a day."

"Then," said his son, "I will have none of your money," and he, too, tried to get a job on a ferryboat that Saturday night. He could not get one there, but he did get a job for three dollars a week. Of course, if a rich man's son will do that, he will get the discipline of a poor boy that is worth more than a university education to any man. He would then be able to take care of the millions of his father.

But as a rule the rich man will not let his son do the very thing that made him great. As a rule, the rich man will not allow his son to work. And his mother! Why, she would think it was a social disgrace if her poor boy had to earn his living with honest toil. I have no pity for such rich men's sons.

False Eyeglasses

I must tell you about a rich man's son at Niagara Falls. I came in from the lecture to the hotel, and as I approached the desk there stood a millionaire's son from New York. It is a very difficult thing to de-

scribe that young man. He wore an eyeglass that he could not see through, patent-leather boots that he could not walk in, and pants that he could not sit down in—he was dressed like a grasshopper. This human cricket came up to the desk just as I entered, adjusted his unseeing eyeglass, and spoke to the clerk. You see, he thought it was "Hinglish, you know," to lisp. "Thir, will you have the kindness to supply me with thome papah and enwelops!"

The hotel clerk measured that man quickly, and pulled the envelopes and paper out of a drawer, pushed them across the counter toward him, and then turned away to his books.

You should have seen that young man when those envelopes came across the counter. He swelled up like a gobbler turkey, adjusted his unseeing eyeglass, and yelled, "Come right back here! Now thir, will you order a thervant to take that papah and enwelops to yondah dethk."

Oh, the poor, miserable monkey! He could not carry paper and envelopes twenty feet.

If you have not capital, young man, I am glad of it. What you need is common sense, not copper cents.

The Fortunate Failure

The best thing I can do is to illustrate by facts known to you all. A. T. Stewart, a poor boy in New York, had $1.50 to begin life on. He lost 87 1/2 cents of that on his very first venture. How fortunate the young man who loses the first time he gambles.

That boy said, "I will never gamble again in business," and he never did.

How did he lose 87 1/2 cents? You probably know the story how he lost it—because he bought some needles, threads, and buttons to sell which people did not want, and had them left on his hands, a dead loss.

The boy said, "I won't lose any more money that way."

Then he took a survey and asked people what they did want. When he had found out what they wanted he invested his 62 1/2 cents to supply a known demand.

Study it wherever you choose—in business, in your profession, in your housekeeping, whatever your life, that one thing is the secret of success. You must first know the demand. You must first know what people need, and then invest in what is most needed.

A. T. Stewart went on that principle until he was worth forty million dollars, owning the very store Mr. Wanamaker runs in New York.

His fortune was made by his losing something, which taught him the great lesson that he must invest himself or his money in something that people need. When will you salesmen learn it? When will you manufacturers learn that you must know the changing needs of humanity if you would succeed in life? Apply yourselves, all you Christian people, as manufacturers or merchants or workmen to supply human needs. It is a great principle as broad as humanity and as deep as the Scripture itself.

Astor's Secret of Success

The best illustration is the example of John Jacob Astor. He made his money in New York. He came to America in debt. But that poor boy with nothing in his pocket made his fortune on one principle.

Some young man here tonight will say, "Well, he could make a fortune in New York, but he could not do it here!"

My friends, records of 107 millionaires in New York show that only seven made their money there. Out of 107 millionaires worth ten million dollars in real estate, 67 of them made their money in towns of less than 3,500 inhabitants. The richest man in this country today has never moved away from a town of 3,500 inhabitants. It makes no difference where you are, but who you are. For if you cannot get rich here, you certainly cannot get rich in New York.

John Jacob Astor illustrates what can be done anywhere. He had a mortgage once on a millinery store that could not sell bonnets enough to pay the interest on his money. So he foreclosed the mortgage, took possession of the store, and went into partnership with the very same people, in the same store, with the same capital.

He did not give them a dollar of capital. He went out and sat down on a bench in the shade of Central Park. What was John Jacob Astor doing out there, and in partnership with people who had failed? He had the most important and, to my mind, the most pleasant part of that partnership. For as John Jacob Astor sat on that bench he was watching the ladies as they went by. He was studying their bonnets. In John Jacob Astor's day there was an art about the millinery business, and he went back to the millinery store and said, "Now put the bonnets I describe to you into the show window, because I have seen that ladies like them."

Every hat or bonnet in that show window some lady liked before it was made up. That was the beginning of a great store in New York. And so I tell you if a man could foresee the millinery business he could foresee anything under heaven!

Knowing the Need

Young man, remember if you know what people need you have more chances of making a fortune than any amount of capital can give you.

There was a poor man out of work in Hingham, Massachusetts. He lounged around the house until one day his wife told him to get out and work, and, as he lived in Massachusetts, he obeyed his wife. He went out and sat on the shore of the bay, and whittled a soaked shingle into a wooden chain. His children quarreled over it that evening, and he whittled a second one to keep peace.

While he was whittling the second one a neighbor came in and said, "Why don't you whittle toys and sell them? You could make money at it."

"Oh," he said, "I would not know what to make."

"Why don't you ask your own children right here in your own house what to make?"

"What is the use of trying that?" said the carpenter. "My children are different from other people's children."

But he acted upon the suggestion, and the next morning when Mary came down the stairway, he

asked, "What do you want for a toy?" She began to tell him she would like a doll's bed, a doll's washstand, a doll's carriage, a little doll's umbrella, and went on with a list of things that would take him a lifetime to supply.

So, consulting his own children, in his own house, he took the firewood, for he had no money to buy lumber, and whittled those strong, unpainted Hingham toys that were for so many years known all over the world.

That man began to make those toys for his own children, and then made copies and sold them through the boot and shoe store next door. He began to make a little money, and then a little more. That man is worth a hundred million dollars today, and has made it on one principle—that we judge the human heart by ourselves, by our wives or by our children. It is the road to success in manufacturing.

"Oh," but you say, "didn't he have any capital?"

Yes, a penknife, but I don't know that he had paid for it.

Right Under Her Chin

I spoke to an audience in New Britain, Connecticut, and a lady four seats back went home and tried to take off her collar. The collar button stuck in the buttonhole. She threw it out and said, "I am going to get up something better to put on collars."

Her husband said, "After what Conwell said to-night, you see there is a need for an improved collar fastener that is easier to handle. There is a human need; there is a great fortune. Now, then, get up a collar button and get rich."

He made fun of her. When her husband ridiculed her, she made up her mind she would make a better collar button, and when a woman makes up her mind, "she will."

It was that New England woman who invented the snap button which you can find anywhere now. It was first a collar button with a spring cap attached to the outer side. Any of you who wear modern raincoats know the button that simply pushes together, and when you unbutton it you simply pull it apart. That is the button to which I refer, and which she invented. She afterward invented several other buttons, and then invested in more. Today that woman travels abroad every summer in her private yacht—yes, and takes her husband with her!

Now what is the lesson? It is this: I told her then, though I did not know her, what I now say to you, "Your wealth is too near you. You are looking right over it," and she had to look over it because it was right under her chin.

Women Are the Inventors

I read in a newspaper that a woman never invented anything. That newspaper could not appear if women had not invented something. Women, think! You say you cannot make a fortune because you are in some laundry, or running a sewing machine, and yet you can be a millionaire if you will but follow this almost infallible direction.

When you say a woman doesn't invent anything, I ask, who invented the Jacquard loom that wove every stitch you wear? Mrs. Jacquard. The printer's roller and the printing press were invented by farmers' wives.

Who invented the cotton gin? Mrs. General Greene invented the cotton gin and showed the idea to Mr. Whitney, and he, just like a man, seized it. Who was it that invented the sewing machine? If I would go to school tomorrow and ask your children they would say, "Elias Howe."

He was in the Civil War with me, and often in my tent, and I heard him say that he spent fourteen years trying to develop a sewing machine. But his wife made up her mind one day that they would starve to death if there wasn't something or other invented pretty soon, and so in two hours she invented the sewing machine. Of course he took out the patent in his name. Men always do that.

Who invented the mower and the reaper? According to a recently published interview with Mr. Mc-Cormick, it was a West Virginia woman. After Mr. McCormick and his father had failed altogether in making a reaper and gave it up, she took a lot of shears and nailed them together on the edge of a board. Then she wired them so that when she pulled the wire one way it closed them, and when she pulled the wire the other way it opened them. And there she had the principle of the mowing machine. If you look at a mowing machine, you will see it is nothing but a lot of shears.

If a woman can invent a mowing machine, if a woman can invent a Jacquard loom, if a woman can invent a cotton gin, if a woman can invent a trolley switch—as one did; if a woman can invent, as Mr. Carnegie said, the great iron squeezers that laid the foundation of all the steel millions of the United States, "we men" can invent anything under the stars! I say that for the encouragement of the men.

Greatness Is Close to You

Who are the great men of the world? Again this lesson comes before us. The great man sits next to you, or you are the person yourself.

The really great man is a plain, straightforward, everyday, common-sense man. You would not dream that he was great if you did not see something he had actually done. His neighbors do not regard him as great. You never see anything great over your back fence. You say there is no greatness among your neighbors. It is all away off somewhere else. Their greatness is ever so simple, so plain, so earnest, so practical, that the neighbors and friends never recognize it.

Let me give you an example. One of my soldiers in the Civil War had been sentenced to death, and I went up to the White House in Washington—sent there for the first time in my life—to see the President. I went into the waiting room and sat down with a lot of others on the benches, and the secretary asked one after another to tell him what they wanted. After the secretary had been through the line, he went in, and then came back to the hall door and motioned for me.

I went up and the secretary said: "That is the President's door right over there. Just rap on it and go right in." I never was so taken aback, friends—never. The secretary himself made it worse for me, because he had told me how to go in and then went out another door and shut that. There I was, in the hallway by myself before the door of the President of the United States of America.

I never was so afraid when the shells came around us at Antietam as I was when I went into that room that day; but I finally mustered the courage—I don't know how I ever did—and at arm's length tapped on

48

the door. The man inside did not help me at all, but yelled, "Come in and sit down!"

Lincoln's Rule for Greatness

Well, I went in and sat on the edge of a chair, and wished I were in Europe. The man at the table did not look up. He was one of the world's greatest men, and was made great by one single rule. Abraham Lincoln's principle for greatness can be adopted by nearly all. This was his rule: Whatever it was he had to do, he put his whole mind into it and held it all there until it was done. That makes men great almost anywhere. He stuck to those papers at that table and did not look up at me, and I sat there trembling. Finally, when he had put a string around his papers, he pushed them over to one side and looked at me, and a smile came over his worn face.

He said, "I am a very busy man and have only a few minutes to spare. Now tell me in the fewest words what it is you want."

I began to tell him, and mentioned the case, and he said, "I have heard all about it and you need not say any more. Mr. Stanton was talking to me only a few days ago about it. You can go to the hotel and rest assured that the President never has signed an order to shoot a boy under twenty years of age, and never will."

Then he said to me, "How is it going in the field?"

I said, "We sometimes get discouraged."

And he said, "It is all right. We are going to win out now. We are getting very near the light. No man should wish to be President of the United States, and I will be glad when I get through. Then Tad and I are going out to Springfield, Illinois. I have bought a farm out there and I don't care if I only earn twenty-five cents a day. Tad has a mule team, and we are going to plant onions."

Then he asked me, "Were you brought up on a farm?"

I said, "Yes; in the Berkshire Hills of Massachusetts."

He then threw his leg over the corner of the big chair and said, "I have heard many a time, since I was young, that up there in those hills you have to sharpen the noses of the sheep so they can get to the grass between the rocks."

He was so familiar, so everyday, so farmer-like, that I felt right at home with him at once.

He then took hold of another roll of paper, and looked up at me and said, "Good morning."

I took the hint and got up and went out. I could not believe I had seen the President of the United States at all.

But a few days later, when still in the city, I saw the crowd pass through the East Room by the coffin of Abraham Lincoln, and when I looked at the up-turned face of the murdered President I felt then that the man I had seen such a short time before, so simple a man, so plain a man, was one of the greatest men that God ever raised up to lead a nation to ultimate liberty. Yet he was only "Old Abe" to his neighbors.

When they had the second funeral, I was invited among others, and went out to see the same coffin put back in the tomb at Springfield. Around it stood

Lincoln's old neighbors, to whom he was just "Old Abe."

Erased His Way to Wealth

Did you ever see a man who struts around altogether too large to notice an ordinary working mechanic? Do you think he is great? He is nothing but a puffed-up balloon, held down by his big feet. There is no greatness there.

Who are the great men and women? My attention was called the other day to the story of a poor man in Massachusetts. He had worked in the nailworks, was injured at thirty-eight, and could earn but little money. He was employed in the office to rub out the marks on the bills made by pencil memorandums, and he used a piece of rubber until his hand grew tired. He then tied the rubber on the end of a stick and worked it like a plane.

His little girl came and said, "Why, you have a patent, haven't you?"

The father said afterward, "My daughter told me when I took that stick and put the rubber on the end of it there was a patent."

He went to Boston and applied for his patent, and every one of you that has a rubber-tipped pencil in your pocket is now paying tribute to that millionaire. No capital, not a penny did he invest in it. All was income, all the way up into the millions.

But there are two other young men here, and that is all I will venture to say, because it is too late. One over there gets up and says, "There is going to be a great man in this city, but never was one." "Oh, is that so? When are you going to be great?" "When I am elected to some political office." Young man, won't you learn a lesson in the primer of politics that it is a *prima facie* evidence of littleness to hold office under our form of government? Great men get into office sometimes, but what this country needs is men that will do what we tell them to do. This nation— where the people rule—is governed by the people, for the people, and so long as it is, then the office-holder is but the servant of the people, and the Bible says the servant cannot be greater than the master. The Bible says, "He that is sent cannot be greater than He who sent him." The people rule, or should rule, and if they do, we do not need the greater men in office. If the great men in America took our of-ices, we would change to an empire in the next ten years.

A young man says, "There are going to be great men in this city."

"Is that so? When?"

"When there comes a great war, when we get into difficulty through watchful waiting in Mexico; when we get into war with England over some frivolous deed, or with Japan or China or New Jersey or some distant country. Then I will march up to the can-non's mouth; I will sweep up among the glistening bayonets; I will leap into the arena and tear down the flag and bear it away in triumph. I will come home with stars on my shoulder, and hold every office in the gift of the nation, and I will be great."

Offices Don't Make Men

No, you won't. You think you are going to be made great by an office, but remember that if you are not great before you get the office, you won't be great when you secure it.

I remember an illustration. I shut my eyes now and look back to my native town in Massachusetts. I can see the Congregational church; see the town hall and mountaineers' cottages; see a great assembly of people turning out, dressed resplendently, and I can see flags flying and handkerchiefs waving and hear bands playing. I can see a company of soldiers that had re-enlisted marching up.

I was but a boy, but I was captain of that company and puffed out with pride. A needle would have burst me all to pieces. Then I thought it was the greatest event that ever came to man on earth.

The bands played, and all the people turned out to receive us. I marched up that common so proud at the head of my troops, and we turned into the town hall. Then they seated my soldiers down the center aisle and I sat down on the front seat.

A great assembly of people—a hundred or two— came in to fill the town hall, so that they stood up all around. Then the town officers came in.

The mayor of the town sat in the middle of the platform. He was a man who had never held office before; but he was a good man. He was a good man, but he thought an office made a man great. He came up and took his seat, adjusted his powerful spectacles, and looked around, when he suddenly spied me sitting there on the front seat. He then came forward on the platform and invited me to sit with the town officers.

No town officer ever took any notice of me before I went to war, except to advise the teacher to thrash me, and now I was invited up on the stand with the town officers.

Example of an Error

When I was seated, the mayor went forward to the table. We all supposed he would introduce the Congregational minister, who was the only orator in town, and that he would give the oration to the returning soldiers. But, friends, you should have seen the surprise when the audience discovered that the old fellow was going to deliver the speech himself. He had never made a speech in his life and he fell into the same error that hundreds of other men have fallen into. He thought all he had to do was hold office to be an orator.

He came up, and brought with him a speech which he had learned by heart walking up and down the

pasture. He brought the manuscript with him and spread it out on the table so as to be sure he could see it. He adjusted his spectacles and leaned over it for a moment and marched back on the platform, and then came forward—tramp, tramp, tramp. He must have studied the subject a great deal, when you come to think of it, because he assumed an "elocutionary" attitude. He rested heavily upon his left heel, threw back his shoulders, and slightly advanced his right foot at a forty-five degree angle. As he stood in that elocutionary attitude, friends, this is just the way his speech went. Some people say to me, "Don't you exaggerate?" That would be impossible. But I am here for the lesson and not for the story, and this is the way it went:

"Fellow-citizens—" As soon as he heard his voice his knees began to shake, and then he trembled all over. He choked and swallowed and came around to the table to look at the manuscript.

Then he gathered himself up with clenched fists and came back: "Fellow-citizens, we are—Fellow-citizens, we are—we are—we are—we are—we are —we are very happy—we are very happy—we are very happy. We are very happy to welcome back to their native town these soldiers who have fought and bled—and come back again to their native town. We are especially—we are especially—we are especially. We are especially pleased to see with us today this young hero"—(that meant me)—"this young hero who in imagination"—(friends, remember he said that; if he had not said "in imagination" I would not be egotistic enough to refer to it at all)— "this young hero who in imagination we have seen leading—we have seen leading—leading. We have seen leading his troops on to the deadly breach. We have seen his shining—we have seen his shining— his shining—his shining sword—flashing. Flashing in the sunlight, as he shouted to his troops, 'Come on'!"

Oh dear, dear, dear! how little that good man knew about war. If he had known anything about war at all he should have known that it is next to a crime in time of danger for an officer of infantry to go ahead of his men. "I, with my shining sword flashing in the sunlight, shouting to my troops, 'Come on'!" I never did it.

Every Officer Has His Place

Do you suppose I would get in front of my troops to be shot in front by the enemy and in the back by my own men? That is no place for an officer. The place for the officer in actual battle is behind the line. The higher the officer's rank the farther behind he goes. Not because he is any the less brave, but because the laws of war require it. And yet he shouted, "I, with my shining sword."

In that house there sat the company of my soldiers. Some of their comrades had gone to death under the shell-swept pines in the mountains of Tennessee, yet in the good man's speech they were scarcely known. He did refer to them, but only incidentally.

The hero of the hour was this young officer. Did the nation owe him anything? No, nothing then and nothing now. Why was he the hero? Simply because the mayor had fallen again into his error of greatness—he considered this boy to be great because he was an officer and these were only private soldiers.

Oh, I learned the lesson then. Greatness consists not in the holding of some future office, but consists in doing great deeds with little means and the accomplishment of vast purposes from the private ranks of life. To be great at all one must be great here, now.

He who can give to this city better streets and better sidewalks, better schools and more colleges, more happiness and more civilization, more of God, he will be great anywhere.

Let every man or woman here, if you never hear me again, remember this, that if you wish to be great, you must begin where you are and with what you are, now. He who can give to his city any blessing, he who can be a good citizen while he lives here, he who can make better homes, he who can be a blessing whether he works in the shop or sits behind the counter or keeps house, whatever be his life, he who would be great anywhere must first be great in his own community. Right here. Right now.

The designer gratefully acknowledges the assistance of Mr. Albert R. Carlisle, Director, Office of Public Information, Temple University, Philadelphia, Pennsylvania, in preparing this book.
Set in Linotype Aldus, a roman with old-face characteristics, designed by Hermann Zapf.
Aldus was named for the 16th century Venetian printer Aldus Manutius.
Typography by Grant Dahlstrom, set at The Castle Press.
Printed on Hallmark Eggshell Book paper.
Designed by Harald Peter.